winning
boxing

winning boxing

Julius McClure "Kid" Carson
with Lacy Banks

Contemporary Books, Inc.
Chicago

Library of Congress Cataloging in Publication Data

Banks, Lacy, 1943-
   Winning boxing.

   Includes index.
   1. Boxing.   I. Title.
GV1133.B36   796.8'3   79-22022
ISBN 0-8092-7152-4
ISBN 0-8092-7151-6 pbk.

Copyright © 1980 by Lacy Banks
All rights reserved
Published by Contemporary Books, Inc.
180 North Michigan Avenue, Chicago, Illinois 60601
Manufactured in the United States of America
Library of Congress Catalog Card Number: 79-22022
International Standard Book Number: 0-8092-7152-4 (cloth)
                                     0-8092-7151-6 (paper)

Published simultaneously in Canada by
Beaverbooks
953 Dillingham Road
Pickering, Ontario L1W 1Z7
Canada

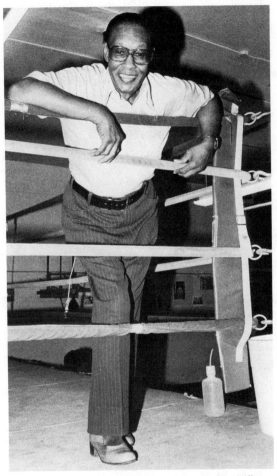

Photo by Chuck Kirman

Shortly after the completion of this book, Julius McClure "Kid" Carson, seventy-two, died following a long bout with cancer. "It's a great loss for boxing," said Muhammad Ali. "Carson was one of the best trainers in the game. He was also a good man and a friend." Mrs. Nellie Mildred Carson, Kid's wife of thirty-four years, heads a legion of surviving relatives and friends. This book, then, is in part a monument to Carson, who spent close to half a century training some of the best fighters of all time.

contents

foreword
by muhammad ali

I started boxing when I was twelve years old in Louisville, Kentucky. Somebody stole my bicycle, and I went into the police station where this patrolman named Joe Martin was. He helped train guys to become boxers. I was crying and mad and ready to beat up the guy who stole my bike. I became a fighter because of that.

I won my first two amateur fights, lost the third one. All were three-round bouts. I started out being successful; so I liked the feel of victory. I liked the idea of being on television; it gave me the drive to go. I wasn't fighting for money at the time. I was fighting just for fame. I liked the idea of being famous. I liked the idea of being on television and all my high school classmates telling me that they saw me there.

Then one night after leaving the training center at Columbia Gym in Louisville, Kentucky—it was a rainy night, I was riding my bicycle, and Rocky Marciano had just knocked out Jersey Joe Walcott or somebody—I could still hear in my mind part of the radio broadcast:

"The winner, and still heavyweight champion of the world, Rocky Marciano!"

All the way home, I heard that in my mind: " . . . still heavyweight champion of the world." As a little boy in Louisville, just being the champion of the state of Kentucky was a dream come true. Louisville was a big place to a little boy like me. But now my mind turned toward being heavyweight champion of the world. And that became my new drive. I wanted to one day hear the man call me the heavyweight champion of the world.

Well, I've heard that not just once but three times. They've ranked me greater than Rocky Marciano, greater than Jack Johnson, greater than Jersey Joe Walcott, greater than Sugar Ray Robinson—the greatest of all times! But I can still trace my world championships back to where I started. If I had to pinpoint one thing that made me the greatest, it would be the mind and the willpower to be a winner. My determination as a fighter was always to be successful. I set my goal, and I went right to it. And that's the first thing I'd tell you young fighters coming up. If you want to be a winner, first thing to do is to make up your mind that you're going to win regardless of what anybody anywhere ever says or does. Be determined to be successful.

Very often we find out that a man who has a successful start in life—he goes on being successful. And the man who once fails seems to go on failing. Why? Looked at from the psychological point of view, the successful man was impressed in his mind by success and branded with it; so he continues to be successful. The man who failed was branded in his mind with failure; so he continues to fail. His early failure suggested to him that he would always be a failure, and he let that idea become branded into his mind.

But it's not because of the displeasure of God that unfortunate souls continue to be unfortunate in all they do. It is the suggestion of misery, it is the suggestion of misfortune, that keeps them miserable throughout their lives.

I once heard a story about a rich man who had lost all his money. His name was Muhammad Ali. He lost his money fighting the draft. Yet I wouldn't admit I was a failure. People— and it sometimes seemed like the whole world—laughed at me, said I was finished, counted me out. But I said, "No! I'm still the champion! I'm still the greatest! I still got my money somewhere in my mind."

And within three and a half years, I was richer than ever before. And anybody who fought me became a rich man. Why? Because I never allowed failure to suggest itself to me.

"Winning! Winning!" That's what I thought and that's how I talked. "I'm the champ, not the tramp! I'm beautiful!" These are good things to think of yourself.

Often people will say, after they've forgotten something in life—which is a perfectly natural thing for a human being to do—"How stupid on my part!" or "How forgetful I am!" But repeating this idea only deepens their stupidity, deepens their forgetfulness.

There are many drawbacks in life—in sports, in boxing, in everything—as when a person says, "When I'm among people, I get timid; I become nervous. When I'm asked to speak or do something, I can't do it." All these are bad suggestions. We should never allow the spirit of misery and defeat—which are in all of us—to be strengthened by thoughts and feelings of inability. The essence of life is hope. Hope you'll be better and ye shall be better.

Hopelessness is worse than death. It is better to die than to lose hope and give up. This is the attitude I've had through all my boxing. I started out successful and I stayed successful. And I always thought of myself—and still do—as the winner. Some of the fighters who started boxing when I did—they started out failing, and they continued failing because they allowed failure to suggest itself to them.

I want to thank Kid Carson and Lacy Banks and wish them good luck on this book they're doing with tips of mine included.

Lacy is a great writer. I met him when he was at *Ebony* and I was training for my first fight with Joe Frazier. We spent a lot of time together.

Kid is a great trainer. He was one of my trainers when I was in exile. He worked with me and helped me keep in shape. He knows boxing. And to have all his knowledge behind me—all that rich know-how dating back to Jack Johnson, one of the greatest fighters besides myself—helped give me the edge on the other guys when I came back.

I have so many followers. Like I followed Joe Louis when I was coming up. And if Joe had told me how to run and how to eat, I would have actually done those things. That's what makes this book so great: there are many questions in the minds of fighters who would like to be like Muhammad Ali; here, they can read my very words and hear what I have to say about it.

introduction

I compiled a seventy-five and twenty-five won-loss record as a pro lightweight in the early twenties before quitting because I wasn't making enough money. I decided to train boxers, and that has been my greatest glory. Among the hundreds of fighters I've worked with as trainer have been seven world champions.

They are: Jack Johnson, who in 1908 became the first black to win the world heavyweight title; Eddie Perkins, who won the world junior welterweight title in 1963; Freddie Little, who won the world junior middleweight title on March 17, 1969; Johnny Bratton, who won the National Boxing Association welterweight championship on March 14, 1951; Joe Brown, who won the world lightweight title in 1956; Ernie Terrell, World Boxing

Julius McClure Carson, the man Jack Johnson nicknamed "Kid" because he was "quick on the draw" as a trainer, has been training fighters for more than forty years. (Photo by Chuck Kirman)

Association heavyweight champion in 1965; and Muhammad Ali, three-time world heavyweight champion.

I'm now in my forty-seventh year of training boxers. I'm not training as much as I used to; old age and arthritis have combined to slow me down. But I still train a few around Chicago and am the trainer-manager of an excellent light heavyweight prospect named Julius Noble.

Training boxers has been my life for some time now. It is the only thing I know how to do, and if I didn't do it I'd die watching walls close in on me. I want to share what knowledge I've acquired with the young boxers—help keep kids out of trouble and help young men's championship dreams come true—so I go to the gym every day, and I get after the fighter who is not putting his weight behind his punches or who is dropping his arm after he jabs.

Anyway, boxing has been extremely good to me. I've worked with the best the ring has had to offer. It has enabled me to travel around the world several times. It's given me sweet memories to enjoy the rest of my life. And even if I train fighters free for a hundred more years, I still won't be able to repay boxing for what it has given me.

JULIUS McCLURE "KID" CARSON

winning
boxing

chapter one

basic boxing decisions

During my fourteen years as a fighter and more than forty-five years as a trainer of hundreds of boxers, I've seen many, many changes in the sport. I've seen changes in its material equipment, changes in its champions, changes in its fighting styles, changes in its popularity, and changes in its payment of fighters. But the basic decisions that must be made before one becomes a boxer remain the same. Let's consider the two principal ones.

The first basic decision ideally should be a joint one: you and a qualified physician must agree that your decision to be an amateur boxer is justified by your health. There are many of you with sufficient desire, mental ability, and fundamental physical skills to make excellent boxers. But if you have a weak heart or

The decision to be a winning boxer is the decision to work hard, master the basics of boxing, maintain top physical condition, and do your best offensively and defensively each time you fight. If you do these things, your arms will be raised in victory after many a fight.

have suffered a skull or brain injury, boxing could endanger your life. Many of you may feel healthy. But because a medical examination may reveal otherwise, it is important that you get one to be sure of your health.

In fact, when you apply for your amateur license, you must pass a physical examination. Then, when you apply for your professional license, along with your birth certificate, amateur record, and two passport-size portraits, you must provide evidence of an electrocardiogram, chest x-ray, blood test, plus a written report and approval from your personal physician. Then, before every professional fight, you must undergo a physical examination by the physician representing your state athletic board.

Your second basic decision is whether you want to box to win or box for one of several other reasons. Legendary football coach Vince Lombardi reportedly believed, "Winning is not everything, it's the only thing." I disagree. In boxing, I believe winning is neither everything nor the only thing. But for the typical fighter, winning *is* the ultimate aspiration—especially if he is poor. Boxing traditionally has been the poor boy's quick ticket to fame and fortune. But to become a winner and remain one, you must have certain spiritual tools or intangibles. They are the following:

- **Determination**—you've got to be willing to work as hard and as long as it takes to become a winner.
- **Courage**—you can't give in to the fear of losing or getting hurt.
- **Confidence**—your confidence in your ability to win should always be greater than your fears of losing or getting hurt.
- **Trainability**—you must be willing to listen to and follow a trainer's instructions.
- **Discipline**—you must have the willingness to stick to a training schedule.
- **Patience**—you must have the ability to wait, take your time, develop, and move up the competitive scale properly.

5

These are the intangibles a perceptive and responsible trainer should look for in a prospect before making a definite decision to be the prospect's trainer. The trainer eventually learns that by recognizing these things he may save himself and the fighter time, energy, and money.

DISCOURAGEMENT IS FIRST TEST

I first try to talk a young man out of becoming a fighter to test his willpower: you must *want* to fight if you are to succeed. I say, "No! You want to be a fighter? You got to be kidding." Then I tell him about the long hard hours of training and the pain. If he doesn't let me talk him out of boxing, that's a good sign he's serious and determined enough to become a good boxer.

Many young men don't understand how demanding and grueling a sport boxing is. They see boxing on television—see Muhammad Ali shuffle—and think boxing is as easy as it looks. They come into the gym all excited and convinced that they are going to be the next champion of the world. But within six months, half of the prospects I work with end up quitting for one reason or another.

Maybe one of them got hit pretty hard—got the wind knocked out of him and lost the courage to risk being hit again. Or maybe his girlfriend threatened to quit him if he didn't spend more time with her and less in the gym. Maybe he found the going too rough—training regularly to get in shape and stay in shape. Maybe he wanted to become champion overnight and became impatient and discouraged when he didn't. Such a fighter lacks the intangibles essential to winning. Unfortunately, by the time this is realized, he may have spent a good deal of money on equipment, or gotten promoters and managers to invest big money developing him.

Don't buy a lot of equipment until you know what becoming a winning boxer involves and are sure you want to pay the price. Don't let eager relatives or professional sponsors, like managers, try to make up your mind for you or prematurely spend a lot of money on you. I've seen a lot of fighters destroyed in this way. They get too much too soon, get the big head, fail to be realistic about themselves, their ability, and their commitment.

BOOT CAMP AUDITION

I try to help a prospect see the light early. I take my time. If I fail to talk him out of boxing, then I give him a real indication of what boxing is about by sending him through three or four weeks of what the military calls basic training, or boot camp.

I provide everything except mouthpiece and inexpensive gym shoes and clothes. I have the prospect jog two miles a day. Then I have him come into the gym, loosen up by moving around the ring, exercise, shadow box, and learn basic defense against punches.

After four weeks of this, I have an experienced fighter get into the ring and spar with him to see how well the prospect has learned to block punches. His mistakes, of course, can be painful, but they serve to show him how demanding and serious a business boxing is.

By this time, the prospect should have discovered for himself whether he's willing to do the hard training required of a winning boxer. If he isn't, he'll quit on his own and save the trainer the job of embarrassing him. This is good because it is a decision that the fighter should make anyway: no trainer should; no trainer is perfect.

But the prospect should be given the opportunity to see first-hand what boxing is all about so that he will be able to make a responsible decision about his own future.

chapter two

the equipment

When it is reasonably certain that the prospect has the talent and desire to be a boxer, then it is time to advise him to buy his own boxing equipment. The YMCAs, Boys Clubs, Police Athletic Leagues, Park Districts, Catholic Youth Organizations, and private gyms where fighters generally start will normally furnish the major hardware, such as the ring (which may range in size from sixteen feet square to twenty-four feet square), heavy punching bag, exercise equipment, and some of the smaller personal equipment. But the boxer definitely should purchase the personal equipment he wears, such as the mouthpiece, boxing shoes, training gloves, speedbag, protective foolproof cup, skipping rope, jogging suit, socks, headguard, handwraps,

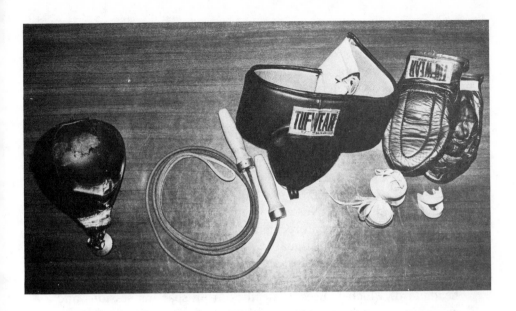

Basic training and fighting equipment includes *(above, from left)* speed bag, skipping rope, protective foolproof cup, handwraps, training gloves, mouthpiece, *(below, from left)* punching ball (optional item), headguard, and sparring gloves.

trunks for training and fighting (usually colorful satin trunks), and robe (also preferably of satin for fights and of cotton for training).

PROTECTIVE GEAR

Like other sports featuring aggressive physical contact, boxing entails risks of personal injury. But injuries are minimized when fighters wear protective equipment and when there is close medical scrutiny and enforcement of boxing rules.

The mouthpiece, headguard, various gloves, protective fool-proof cup, and handwraps are all aimed at protecting various parts of the fighter's body from injury. With the exception of the headguard, which is used basically during sparring sessions and exhibitions, a fighter should use these items at all times.

It is no real badge of courage for any fighter to train or fight without the proper protective gear. Instead it is both a sign of foolishness and it is a violation of rules set by responsible gyms and boxing commissions. Some of this gear, such as the mouthpiece and protective foolproof cup, may feel a little awkward at times. But they are built for safety, not for comfort and convenience. Use them!

The Mouthpiece

Roughly ninety percent of all knockouts are caused by shots to the head. Thus, the mouthpiece may be the most important safety item because it is used to protect the mouth and jaws. But often, during sparring sessions and actual matches, fighters will spit out their mouthpieces to facilitate breathing or, on occasion, to try to intimidate the opponent by implying that they aren't being hit hard enough to need the mouthpiece. This is danger-ous. For one thing, a fighter can step on a mouthpiece, slip, fall and injure himself. But more important, he increases the risk of serious damage to the mouth and jaw. A fighter's teeth can be knocked out even when he wears a mouthpiece. So without a mouthpiece, any half-decent punch or mild butt can cause a fighter to break his jaw, get his teeth knocked out, damage his gums, bite his lip or tongue.

A broken jaw is a very serious injury and usually results in a loss for the injured fighter. The pain is simply unbearable and the fighter greatly weakens his defense while trying to protect his broken jaw from additional punches. That's the main reason Ken Norton was able to upset Muhammad Ali in their first fight in San Diego, 1973: Norton broke Ali's jaw in the middle of their twelve-round bout. Ali managed to finish the fight, but conceded so many rounds while trying to protect his jaw that Norton won a unanimous decision.

The mouthpiece helps prevent the broken jaw by bracing the jaws and keeping them from sliding too far apart when a fighter is hit on the chin. The mouthpiece also helps minimize the chances of a fighter losing his teeth, or damaging his gums, lips, or tongue. The latter three injuries usually cause a lot of blood to flow which, when mixed with saliva, gives the fighter more to swallow, makes it harder for him to breathe through his mouth, and makes it easier for him to choke.

Mouthpieces generally are made of hard rubber or plastic, and come in various shapes and sizes; but they normally leave enough room for a fighter to breathe sufficiently through his mouth. And they certainly don't interfere with his breathing through his nose. You should breathe through the nose anyway. If you can't breathe through your nose because it is bleeding too badly or because it is broken, then you should not be fighting. It's best your trainer stop the fight rather than aggravate the injury and make complete healing almost impossible.

The Headguard

The headguard cushions the head against punches and butts and is normally used during sparring sessions and exhibitions. Wear it!

For reasons of hygiene and because headguards come in different sizes, the fighter should purchase his own. Make sure the headguard fits and is neither too tight nor too loose.

11

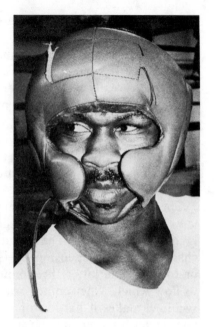

Headguards protect the head from injury during sparring sessions and exhibition matches. They come in different styles and sizes; so get your own.

A headguard that is too tight can interfere with blood circulation to the brain; this is extremely dangerous. Decreased blood flow to the brain dulls and slows a fighter's reflexes, makes him dizzy and sleepy. In the ring, where speed, quickness, and mental alertness are invaluable, a fighter can never afford to be groggy and dizzy.

A headguard that is too loose will slide easily over the eyes, obstruct vision, and make a fighter vulnerable to blows he otherwise would not suffer.

Today's headguards protect better than ever before because of new stuffing. Years ago, the headguard was stuffed with horsehair, which proved harmful because the hard sharp fibers could stick through the leather cover and could get into fighters' eyes or be inhaled through their noses. Horsehair also lacked resilience, thus offering little cushioning of blows. The head absorbed all the impact of the punch. Today's headguards are stuffed with foam rubber, giving them more bounce and cushion than ever before.

The Gloves

Gloves, like headguards and protective cups, also were formerly stuffed with horsehair, but today are stuffed with foam rubber. Padded even more by fighters' handwraps, gloves help minimize damage not just to the hands but to whatever part of the body is punched.

The three basic kinds of gloves are training gloves, sparring or exhibition gloves, and official boxing gloves. Training gloves used for working out on speed bag and heavy bag weigh about four ounces. Actual boxing gloves range in weight from six to fourteen ounces.

It's good for a fighter to have his own training and fighting gloves. But gloves for official amateur and professional fights are provided by promoters and approved by the local boxing commission. For title fights, the boxing commission provides gloves. For all fights other than title fights, the fighters normally wear their gloves into the ring. For title matches, the fighters have their gloves fitted in the ring.

The Handwraps

The handwraps, which are made of cotton or synthetic fiber, pad and protect the fighter's knuckles and wrists. However, the handwraps must be wound around the wrists and hands properly to do their jobs.

Fighters should learn how to tape their own hands.

13

Punching must be done with a tightly clenched fist, so the hand must be wrapped in a way that allows this. At the same time, the wrap must be snug and secure enough not to easily slip or come loose as the fighter punches. The wrists must be wrapped firmly to prevent sprains.

Trainers usually wrap their fighter's hands, but the fighter should be able to wrap his own since he may often have to do so. For training sessions, fighters purchase single-strip handwraps that can be used again and again. For official fights, though, gauze and tape are used, and the wrapping is checked and approved by boxing commission officials to prevent illegal overwrapping. For example, overwrapping knuckles with excessive tape; this gives the fists hitting hardness slightly short of brass knuckles.

Foolproof Cup

Blows below the belt are illegal, but often a punch will land in that area. The protective foolproof cup helps minimize damage caused by such blows. The cup may be worn over the trunks during practice sessions so that it can be easily pulled on and off as a fighter moves back and forth from the ring to the exercise floor. In official fights, however, the leathered, foam-rubber-filled cup is worn under the trunks.

Injuries caused by below-the-belt punches are serious, since a fighter can suffer irreparable damage to reproductive organs. Always wear the cup in the ring.

SHOES

The boxing shoes are traditionally high-topped to help support the ankles and prevent twists and sprains. They should be as lightweight as possible to facilitate footwork. But they should not be so slick on the sole that the fighter will be slipping off balance and setting himself up for a knockout or for a pulled or strained ankle or leg. Balance is extremely important to a fighter's effectiveness. And although slick-bottomed shoes may make it easier for a fighter to do the "Ali shuffle," they may make it harder for him to stay on his feet and win the fight.

A pair of heavy combat or hunting boots are preferred for roadwork. Jogging in heavy boots helps minimize injuries to feet and ankles. Wear thick socks, maybe even two or three pairs to cushion and insulate feet against blisters. Running in heavy boots strengthens the ankles and legs and makes feet quicker in light boxing shoes.

If feet become too tender during the early phase of roadwork, a pair of thick-soled jogging shoes should be used until feet heal and toughen. The jogging boom has encouraged the production of high-quality jogging shoes at low prices.

Traditionally, boxing shoes are made of leather and are high-topped to give ankles extra support.

LUBRICATING SUBSTANCE

Fighters should use petroleum jelly or any comparable lotion to lubricate skin areas that are frequently rubbed, thus preventing burns and blisters. Such key areas include:

- Groin region where straps on athletic supporter and protective foolproof cup rub a lot during leg movement.
- Bottom of feet where blisters can result from roadwork.
- Around eyes, mouth, nose, and ears where friction with boxing gloves can result in cuts.
- Around waist where constant rubbing by trunks and/or protective cup girdle can cause bruises.

chapter three

trainer and manager—
do you need them

Rev. Bob Richards, Olympic gold medal pole vaulter, used to
promote a certain cereal with a proverb that holds true for
boxing: Champions are made, not born.

A lot of science and hard work and discipline go into winning
boxing. And boxing is too lonely and too demanding a sport for
a fighter to try to make it to the top alone. In fact, no boxer
ever has done so. There are too many papers to sign, too many
important things to keep track of. Every champion has always
had at least a team of two as an amateur and a team of three as
a professional to help him become a winner.

Kid Carson has trained thousands of boxers, including seven
world champions. Standing behind him are *(right)* Eddie Perkins,
who became World Boxing Association junior welterweight champion in 1963, and *(left)* Julius Noble, light heavyweight contender
who well may be the last fighter Carson will train. "You got to
have a good trainer to be a winner," says Perkins. "I couldn't have
made it to the top without Carson's help."

18

TRAINER—TEAMMATE AND COACH

As a fighter, your first teammate is your trainer who, by his role, actually serves as coach. It is the trainer who teaches and preaches the science of winning boxing. He directs the hard work that leads to winning boxing and demands the discipline that assures and insures it.

Your trainer should be someone you trust and someone who looks after your best interest. Once you lose trust in your trainer and become uncomfortable with him, you should try to get another trainer. To go into the ring frustrated and angry because of conflict with your trainer is asking to get knocked out. Your mind won't be totally on the fight. A lot of would-be winning fighters have become losers because of this type of conflict.

Your trainer should be knowledgeable in the fundamentals of boxing. To be sure, it is best that he be a veteran or former boxer himself so that when he speaks, he speaks from first-hand experience as well as of time-honored theory.

It should be a trainer who helps you to make the decision to become a boxer in the first place. Then, when you start, your trainer outlines the training program that will systematically develop you physically, spiritually, mentally, and socially to make that great climb to the top.

TRAINER HELPS WITH POLITICS

I love boxing, but there's a lot of politics and there is some corruption in boxing. This must be acknowledged in my instruction to you about how to become a winner, because most of you fighters will not get the fights that will move you to the top unless certain strings are pulled. You may have championship talent, and you may have an excellent record, but you must either know somebody yourself or have somebody representing you who knows how to negotiate with promoters and other individuals for the fights that will take you to the top.

Often, I see talented fighters become frustrated because they are not moving up. They use the cliché "Won't nobody fight

19

me." If you have a good trainer, you are at least going to get some fights.

As a fighter you have enough to worry about just training, getting in shape, and staying in shape for the fight. It helps to have somebody looking out for you in areas such as matchmaking to insure that you won't be moved too rapidly, placed in a match where you're outclassed, and whipped.

The longer you are undefeated the bigger an attraction you become. As an undefeated boxer you will draw the crowds, the press, and financial backers if you're a pro. The longer you remain undefeated, the better your chances will be of moving into contention.

All the world loves a winner. With a good trainer, you can better your chances of becoming one quicker and being one longer than you would otherwise. Without one, you're at the mercy of promoters who are out to push either their own fighters—whom they manage under someone else's name since it's illegal for promoters to be managers—or fighters belonging to other managers and trainers who are friends of the promoter.

TRAINER MAPS OUT STRATEGY

The trainer normally is your chief strategist for a fight. He should secure whatever information he can about your opponent—his strengths and weaknesses—and inform you what battle plan you must use to win.

The strategy sessions start in training camp. The trainer talks to you, tells you what to expect from your foe, and employs sparring partners to portray your opponent. Today, motion picture photography has made strategy-planning sessions a lot more sophisticated and efficient than they were when I was coming up. With films of your opponent (or someone whose style resembles his), you can better understand the actual fighting style you'll be up against and visualize ways to counter it.

Trainers can have films made of your own performances, and use them to help you critique yourself and correct apparent mistakes. Films also help fighters learn the moves and techniques of the best the ring has had to offer. Films of fights featuring Muhammad Ali, Joe Frazier, Sugar Ray Robinson, Jack Dempsey, Rocky Marciano, and Floyd Patterson are available at low prices for fighters to study style.

MANAGER FOR PROS

As a professional fighter, you will need a trainer and a manager. While the trainer works to develop you as a fighter, the manager works to get you the kinds of fights and the kinds of purses that you deserve.

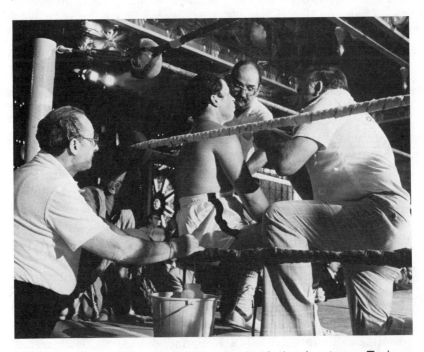

Fighter, trainer, and manager are the basic boxing team. Trainer and manager often act as seconds and tend to their fighter between rounds. Trainer develops fighter physically and emotionally. Manager develops fighter competitively and financially by setting up proper matches.

21

The manager's role is a key one since the fights he sets up can lead to world championships and multimillion-dollar earnings. The manager normally will finance your initial training expenses in return for a certain percentage of your purses over a certain number of years. Your arrangement with your manager is usually structured by a written contract.

Often, you will find fighters using their trainers also as managers. This is done to minimize expense and margin for error and—well, let's say it—the risk of a double cross.

As I said earlier, there is a lot of politics and corruption involved in boxing, but that's understandable since this business involves many millions of dollars in purses every year. Many managers have been accused of pimping for certain promoters by selling out their fighter's best interest when big money is involved. Therefore, a manager should be someone a fighter trusts. Frustrations over managerial problems have caused many fighters to lose fights they should have won.

ALI, LEONARD—BEST MANAGED

With a good trainer and manager, you have an excellent chance of becoming a champion despite the ruthlessness of promoters. Winning an Olympic gold medal was highly important in boosting Muhammad Ali's career. But what really made him a rich man was the training expertise of Angelo Dundee and the managerial excellence of Herbert Muhammad, not to mention the raw genius of Ali who also had a huge hand in the production and negotiations of his million-dollar fights.

Dundee is now using his experience as trainer-manager to guide the promising career of Sugar Ray Leonard, whom many call the best managed fighter in the world right now. While most of the top fighters of the world presently are the contractual properties of promoters Don King and Bob Arum, Dundee has gone outside them and enabled Leonard to become a winner and a prosperous one through a lush television contract.

Sure, the fact that Leonard won an Olympic gold medal

helped him, too. But there have been many other Olympic gold medalists who have gone downhill after the games because they got hooked up with a lousy trainer or manager or both. Dundee's input was invaluable in helping Leonard get the TV contract, and Dundee monitors the matches Leonard fights to assure that he's not pushed too soon, but moves to higher levels of competition as he progresses in fighting ability.

FATHERS NOT RECOMMENDED

Many fighters turn to their fathers to be their trainers and managers. It's understandable why. They trust their fathers and believe that their fathers won't steal their money. Fathers will look out for them better than anybody else.

But in most cases this does not lead to winning boxing because the fathers look out for their sons a little too well for their sons' own good. A father trainer-manager tends to be either overly protective and sensitive about his son's getting hurt, or overly ambitious about his son's future. After all, the fighter is his own flesh and blood.

The father generally moves his son either too slowly—undermatching him because he does not want him to get hurt; or he moves him too fast—overmatching him because he believes his son is the greatest ever in the world, until the son gets knocked out the first round some night by a fighter the father didn't bother to check out.

The father is not realistic and objective. His match-making decisions are often based on emotion—his great love for and pride in his son. They should be based on the cold recognition of what kind of fighter his son is and what kind of competition he needs at a certain time to advance. By asking for more money than his son is worth, the father trainer-manager sometimes makes it difficult for promoters to use his son. Again, as a father, he's emotional: his son deserves the best, even if he isn't the best. It's not impossible to find a good trainer-manager in your dad. But it is very, very difficult. I don't recommend it.

MOVING THE FIGHTER

A fighter wins and gains a title not just because he has ability, but because somebody knows how to maneuver or "move" him up the ranks. "Moving" a fighter means producing the kinds of matches that he is capable of winning and that will move him up in the ratings. Moving the fighter is the principal responsibility of the trainer, manager, and promoter. They must know the fighter's ability, his progress, the opponents he is capable of beating, and the opponents and styles that should be ducked.

The promoter has a vital role in moving the fighter into title contention. Often doubling as a matchmaker, he promotes the general fight card and the individual fighters. If a trainer and manager don't look out for their fighter, promoters sometimes undermatch or overmatch him to his disadvantage.

For example, managers will avoid setting up matches with left-handed boxers or with boxers who have unorthodox styles. They know that the less confused you are about an opponent's style, the easier it will be for you to win.

If you are a left-handed fighter, you have an advantage, since most fighters are right-handed and accustomed to fighting right-handers. It would not, therefore, be in your favor for your trainer and manager to switch you around to a right-handed stance (right foot out front and jabs leading off right hands). As a left-hander, many fighters may refuse to fight you. But if you win and move up the ranks and become a contender, the champion and the other contenders will have to fight you sooner or later.

By knowing the weaknesses and strengths of you and your opponents, your trainer and manager can decide precisely when you are ready to move from amateur to professional boxing. They subsequently determine when you are ready to graduate from four-rounders to six-rounders, then to eight-rounders, ten-rounders, twelve-rounders, and fifteen-round title fights.

Moving a fighter is a complicated process that can take years. It demands patience, confidence, precise timing, influence with boxing commissions, knowledge of opponents, luck, and a favorable rapport with promoters and managers everywhere.

Yes, it costs managers money to move their fighters. They often have to help sell tickets or put up part of the purse to get out-of-town, big-name fighters, who are on the way down as opponents for their unknown but talented fighters, who are on the way up. Many fighters who gained fame simply by losing to champions demand and get large purses for fighting, and lending credibility to, young title prospects.

GAMBLING SOMETIMES NECESSARY

Muhammad Ali beat Sonny Liston because Ali had developed the ability to beat Liston by the time they fought. If Ali had fought Liston a year or so earlier, the result might have been different. But how was Ali's camp to know when Ali was ready to fight Liston? The answer is that Ali, his trainer, and his manager either had sufficient information to indicate that Liston was beatable, or they simply gambled that Ali would win. This is part of moving a fighter. When there is little or no information available on an opponent, your trainer and manager may have to gamble that you can beat that opponent, in the hope of moving you up the ladder of contention. However, gambling and barnstorming are the worst ways to make a winner. There are a lot of nobodies out there who are better than you. Don't look for them too hard or you'll find them when you've got a 15-0 record and they have a 5-8 record and they may still beat you.

The trainer and manager must be level-headed and unintimidated by public opinion, the press, questionable promoters, and even their own fighters. The trainer and manager may have to resist pressure to develop a fighter too rapidly. Some fighters develop more slowly than others and must be moved more slowly. Others must be moved rapidly to higher levels of competition.

A prejudiced father trainer-manager can harm you as a fighter by consistently protecting you and matching you against inferior opponents. You may compile an impressive but deceptive record—one that does not reflect your true talent. Then when you face a fighter with a comparable record earned against tougher competition, you'll find yourself greatly outclassed and a knockout victim. Fighting mediocre opponents is nothing unusual for beginning fighters.

Theoretically, all beginning fighters are mediocre. But matches against obviously inferior fighters, or "bums" as we call them, fought with the intention of padding your record to develop you as an attraction, will ruin your development as a champion. If you have real championship aspirations, don't be satisfied with being a local attraction. It will help your manager and a promoter make money today, but it can prevent you from making millions as a champion tomorrow. Moreover, you will never know how good you are, or could be, unless you are moved up the competitive ladder properly. If you are winning most all your fights by one-round knockouts, and an unusual number of the guys you are beating are out of shape, don't want to fight, or are even taking ten-counts on their knees, you are probably being exploited as a local attraction. Your manager probably has no intention of making a champion out of you. This doesn't mean that you won't get a shot at being a champion. But it means you will not have developed the talent and experience to make the most of the chance when and if you get it.

FIGHTER HAS VOICE, TOO

This chapter is not meant to imply that the voices of the trainer and manager are absolute. They are human. They make mistakes. I'm simply saying that when a fighter takes off toward a potential multimillion-dollar career, two or three heads are better than one. I'm also saying that when you young fighters start out, you need an old fighter by your side to teach you the trade and to stay on your back and inspire you to do your best. Most of you will half-train, get cheated out of victories or

Learn to listen to your trainer. You may not end up doing every single thing he tells you to do. But learn to listen to the voice of experience before you make your move.

27

Fighters who can't listen to anybody eventually get knocked out.

money, and get tricked into fighting "gorillas" if you don't have a trainer or manager.

But at a certain point, you should be mature enough to have a voice, maybe even the final and decisive voice, in the shaping of your fistic destiny. You must strive to become perceptive enough to sit in the audience, see how fighters perform, and recognize the ones you can beat. You may even ask for fights yourself.

In any case, you should always have the benefit of experienced counsel from your trainer and manager. And a chief characteristic of a winning fighter is that he listens to his trainer and manager and considers their input when he makes a decision. Fighters who don't listen to anybody because they know it all will, sooner or later, see a blurred and hazy figure standing over them, and hear him saying, faintly, " . . . eight, nine, ten. You're out!"

chapter four

training for the fight

From the time a young man asks me to train him to be a boxer and I ask him to get into the ring and shadow box so that I can examine his basic ability to move his body, his training begins. The training program of course is supposed to be outlined by the trainer and is designed to prepare the fighter physically and mentally for a match. Training answers the question of which weight division you will compete in. This is so because ninety percent of the fighters who come into the gym to start training are out of shape and overweight. It is only after they have shed the excess fat and gotten into shape that they can know for sure which weight division is best for them. I've seen guys come into the gym weighing 230 pounds, which is heavyweight size. But

29

once they've finally gotten into tip-top shape, they have occasionally been down to something like 160 pounds, which qualifies them to fight in the middleweight division.

While training, some fighters grow into heavier weight divisions instead of shrinking into lighter ones. For example, Muhammad Ali won an Olympic gold medal as a light heavyweight in 1960. However, by 1964 he had won his first world heavyweight title. Moreover, Floyd Patterson won an Olympic gold medal as a middleweight in 1952 before winning his first world heavyweight crown in 1956.

WEIGHT DIVISIONS

There are thirteen recognized weight divisions:

Heavyweight—over 175 pounds
Light heavyweight—from 161 to 175 pounds
Middleweight—from 155 to 160 pounds
Junior middleweight—from 148 to 154 pounds
Welterweight—from 141 to 147 pounds
Junior welterweight—from 136 to 140 pounds
Lightweight—from 131 to 135 pounds
Junior lightweight—from 127 to 130 pounds
Featherweight—from 123 to 126 pounds
Junior featherweight—from 119 to 122 pounds
Bantamweight—from 113 to 118 pounds
Flyweight—from 109 to 122 pounds
Junior flyweight—not over 108 pounds.

Because there are as many as five weight divisions within fifteen pounds of each other, many fighters are flexible about the division they choose to fight in. One fighter, Henry Armstrong, once held three world championships—featherweight, lightweight, and welterweight—at the same time, winning them all in less than ten months (from October 29, 1937 to August 17, 1938).

Most fighters, however, eventually settle in one weight division. And that's the weight division they qualify for once they are in top physical condition. Choosing a weight division that makes a fighter feel weak, or one that makes him tire too quickly or move too slowly is a sure way to keep him from becoming a winning boxer.

CONDITIONING THE BODY OUTDOORS

Former World Boxing Association heavyweight champion Ernie Terrell says that ninety percent of "winning boxing" is physical conditioning, and that ninety percent of physical conditioning is running. I agree.

Running is widely accepted now as the best conditioner of the body because it exercises and strengthens all the major muscles, including the heart, the legs, stomach, chest, arms, and lungs.

Running is the most comprehensive exercise in your training program. Start out with short distances—a lazy half mile—and gradually build up to about five brisk miles, four or five days a week. Running builds stamina, which proves invaluable in long fights.

31

Running also builds stamina, which is invaluable to a winning boxer. Running is the main part of the fighter's outdoor roadwork. I recommend that fighters start out slowly and jog roughly a mile every other day until they build themselves up to four or five miles, run with ease, every day.

Loosening up with stretching exercises before running and shadow boxing, and breaking into a few windsprints while running, makes the run an even better conditioner.

For running, wear a warm-up suit or old loose clothes. Bundle up in the cold, however, and wear gloves. Don't breathe air that's too cold or run in weather that's too hot; you must be free to run, breathe, and sweat without suffering frostbite or heat stroke. To prevent blisters, lubricate the soles of your feet with a friction-reducing and soothing grease, cream, or lotion and wear thick pairs of socks as a shock-absorbing cushion. Heavy shoes like combat boots are traditionally preferred for roadwork because they make the feet feel lighter once you change into boxing shoes.

When you run is not as important as where. Run where there is plenty of grass or other moderately soft surfaces to prevent strain and shin splints. Run where there is little if any traffic to avoid breathing deadly automotive exhaust fumes. If possible,

Chopping wood is a good outdoor exercise that helps especially to strengthen the arms, shoulders, and wrists. (AP photo)

32

run where it is scenic rather than around a track that forces you to look at the same sights over and over again. Run through neighborhoods, through parks, and countryside. You will be entertained by nature's changing panorama; this will help you to relax and run farther than you otherwise would.

If the weather forbids your running outside, you can still get good exercise running in place in a place as small as your closet. Counting one for each time your left (or right) foot hits the floor, you will run roughly a quarter mile each time your left foot hits 250 times and a mile each time it hits 1,000 times.

Outdoor roadwork is not restricted to running. Performing heavy chores like chopping wood and sawing wood also toughen the body.

GYM WORK MORE STRICT

Outdoor roadwork is normally done early in the morning and is sometimes duplicated in the evening. The indoor gym work usually takes place at midday.

Shadow boxing is usually the first exercise of the gym workout. it is normally done by getting into the ring and going through imaginary moves against an imaginary fighter.

33

Gym work is more diversified and systematic than roadwork. It is an abstract version of an actual fight in that you exercise in sequences of three-minute rounds separated by one-minute pauses.

From the moment you step into the ring to begin your workout with shadow boxing, the trainer has you on the stopwatch. You're in round one and your opponent is invisible, but imagine that he's real. Move around! Imagine him right there before you. Be careful now. He's shooting a jab at you. Duck! He's throwing a straight right. Step back! The left side of his head is open. Hit him with a left hook! He's hurt! Now throw combinations and duck each time he tries to counter. You've hurt him! Knock him out!

After three minutes of this, you'll hear the trainer ring a bell or holler, "Time!" Now you're in between rounds. Relax. But don't slouch. Remember, your opponent is looking at you from his corner. Don't give him an edge by letting him think you're tired. Drink a swallow of water if you need it, or gargle and spit out phlegm. Take a deep breath and walk around a little before the next round.

FROM THE RING TO THE FLOOR

After a couple of rounds of shadow boxing, many trainers will have you spar two or three or four rounds with real fighters. Your workout with sparring partners will be discussed in detail in another chapter.

After the shadow boxing and sparring, you leave the ring to work out on the floor. The first stop is usually the heavy bag. Depending on how many rounds you sparred, you will spend from two to five rounds on the heavy bag.

The trainer is still clocking you and watching you hit the heavy bag, another imagined opponent. You swing with power at the heavy bag, strengthening and sharpening all your punches. The trainer corrects your mistakes, makes sure you put your weight behind them, and cover up after each one. You may swing the bag and circle it, throwing punches at it as you would a moving opponent.

34

Sparring often follows shadow boxing. You mix it up with real opponents, test your reflexes, defense, etc. Some fighters quit after their first sparring session because they realize they don't like the idea of getting hit. Don't try to hurt someone or get hurt while sparring. Save your best for the fight. (Photo by Frank Williams)

The heavy bag develops your heavy punching power—especially hooks, crosses, jabs, and straight hands. Two or three rounds here are sufficient. (Photo by Frank Williams)

35

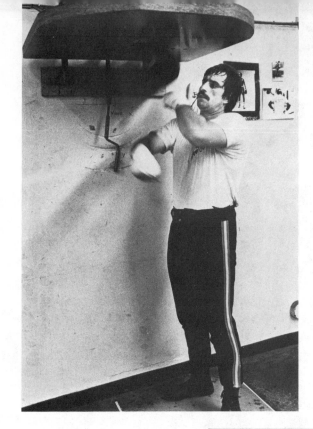

The speed bag develops quick hands and coordination. Two or three rounds are preferred.

Skipping rope is in the same class as running. It builds stamina while developing footwork and body coordination. Two or three rounds of nonstop rope skipping is the minimum for getting in shape. (Photo by Frank Williams)

36

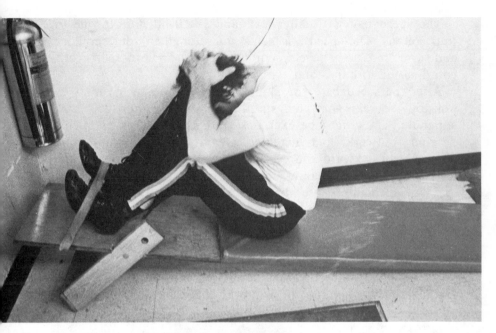

Close out your floor workout with assorted exercises
mixed with shadow boxing.
By now, the sweat should
really be dripping.

37

The speed bag is usually next, and you'll hit it from one to four rounds. The speed bag helps you strengthen your shoulder and arm muscles, develop quick hands, and sharpen your coordination of hands and eyes.

After the speed bag, you skip rope from three to ten minutes nonstop. You can vary your speed from 100 to almost 200 skips a minute. Skipping rope exercises your legs, arms, chest, helps develop footwork, and increases your stamina. Skipping rope may appear awkward and even impossible until you realize that it's just a matter of rhythm—rat-a-tat, rat-a-tat, rat-a-tat.

A lot of fighters use disco music to help them maintain rhythm as they skip. But it's not difficult after you look at the simple bounce of the veteran and imitate it yourself.

After skipping rope, you may close out your gym work with assorted exercises and shadow boxing. Sit-ups, working with the medicine ball, and stretching exercises top off the workout gradually as you cool down to shower and leave.

LIFTING WEIGHTS

I do not strongly recommend weight-lifting unless it is to help strengthen certain muscles in the early stage of a fighter's development. A fighter can actually strengthen his arms and wrists sufficiently for boxing simply through push-ups, chopping and sawing wood, working out on the punching bags, and skipping rope. Lifting weights can add power, but not the thing most important in boxing: stamina. I've seen many muscular, he-man types knocked out by weaker, but faster and quicker, fighters.

A fighter may be extremely strong, but if he is not fast and quick enough to put his power on the target, it won't do him any good. For example, Sonny Liston and George Foreman were much stronger than Muhammad Ali. But Ali had superior quickness and, more important, stamina.

For all his awesome power, Liston could not land a solid blow against dodging, bobbing and weaving Ali. For all his tremendous punching strength, Foreman was an easy prey for knockout punches once he was required to fight beyond the first five or six rounds.

So crucial are speed and quickness that I believe the average pro welterweight fighter (141 to 147 pounds) could beat the average 250-pound pro football player in a fight adhering to official rules.

BREAKING CAMP

Ideally, a training program should be planned so that the fighter reaches his peak at fight time.

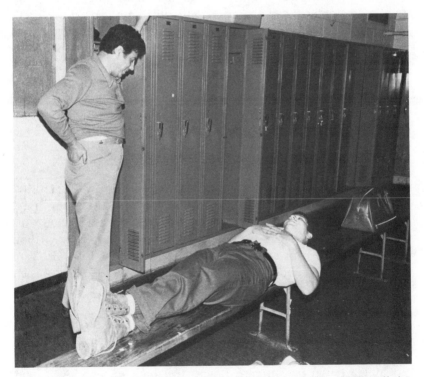

The last two days of camp, take it easy except for some light stretching exercises, breaking a slight sweat. On fight day, you should be at your peak. Arrive early and lie down and relax. Maybe even take a nap.

39

You train until a couple of days before the fight, break camp, do a few stretching exercises to break a sweat those last two days, and on the day of the fight, you're mean and ready to whip the world.

I cannot overemphasize the need to take it easy the last two days before a fight. There is such a thing as overtraining and peaking too soon. I've seen misguided fighters run ten or more miles a day, claiming that they are building their wind. This may be good for marathon running, but this is too much running for the fighter. Fighters who overtrain, subsequently enter the ring tired and weak or fail to show up at all because of a late injury.

Training schedules for roadwork and gym work vary from fighter to fighter. Over the years, a fighter finds a program that's best for him and he sticks with it. Some may spar early, others late, in their gym work. Some may start their workouts on the floor, and end in the ring.

Muhammad Ali's success as a fighter is unquestioned. He is praised by most fight fans and experts as the greatest fighter who ever lived. The following is his advice on training, and a condensation of his training routine for your consideration.

ALI'S TRAINING TIPS

"I always liked to do my roadwork. Running is the main thing, but don't run too much. Try not to run on concrete 'cause it's bad for your legs. Run on soft grass around some park. If you can, find a circle or something that equals a half mile. Get in a car and have somebody measure a certain route and run it. Then mark it with a stone or a tree—remember where the end is so you'll know all the time.

"From age twelve on up to sixteen, three miles of slow jogging with a wind sprint here and there is enough at one time. From age sixteen to twenty, do five miles at the most every day, but do at least two if you can. If you feel bad, do one. And days that you don't feel like running, don't run.

"To do it properly, you've got to go to bed with running in mind. Take your running shoes, your sweat shorts, trunks,

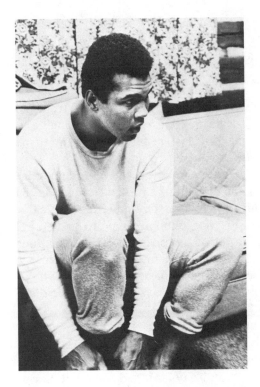

Ali advises that a fighter put his roadwork gear beside his bed and go to bed with running on his mind. That way, he won't have to look for his gear when he gets up the next day and be discouraged from running because he can't find something.

towels and soap—take everything and lay it beside your bed. Psychologically, go to bed with this in mind: 'I'm running in the morning!' Otherwise, when you have to get up and look for things, you'll sometimes find that you've misplaced something; then you'll become discouraged and decide to go back to sleep. You've missed a day of running.

"After running, I'll drink a little water or take some orange juice. Something light. Not much 'cause your body's hot.

"Going to the gym, no later than six P.M. is good for you who still go to school. And get a headstart by walking if you can. I used to walk to the gym a lot. It was about six miles round trip. I was a little tired by the time I got to the gym, but that was good.

"In the gym, two or three rounds on the heavy bag is enough.

41

Two or three rounds on the speed bag. Two or three rounds on the skiprope. Shadow box a round or maybe box two rounds—but not over ten rounds a day, so you have to mix it up. One day you might box three rounds first because you want all your energy for boxing. Then you might go out and work on the heavy bag for three rounds. Or you may push yourself from the floor first: speed bag, rope, heavy bag, shadow boxing, and exercise. Then you get in the ring last because you want to be tired because you want to force yourself to go.

"Here you work on that endurance factor. It's endurance that really counts in a fight. A lot of fighters are great only because they have a great knockout punch. But they must tag you early because they are not really in good enough shape to fight long. If they don't tag you early, a lot of times they'll get knocked out themselves. Endurance helps you outlast fatigue, too. Often in a fight you'll be tired and the other guy will be just as tired: you're going to have to push yourself; and it pays to have been there before—in the gym.

"But don't work too hard in the gym. Don't play around taking a lot of hard punches. Don't get into any fights, and never work with anybody in the gym who hits you too hard. If a man hits you too hard, stop and say, 'Man, look, that hurts! Lighten up!' You're not getting paid for getting beat up in the gym. If you take too many punches in the gym, when fight time comes you're all shook up and beat up. You're too punchy to fight. Your brains are rattled and you're easy to knock out because you wasted all your best in training and didn't save any for the fight."

Ali's Diet Advice

"Eating? Lay off of greasy foods. Eat your meat baked or broiled or boiled: lamb, chicken, fish, veal, or whatever. Steam your vegetables if you can.

"In the morning, toast. Not bread 'cause bread is a little fattening. Watch how you eat in the morning. I'll always eat two or three poached eggs on wheat toast, some sliced tomatoes or something. Or maybe a little cornflakes with some bananas in it first. Then some tea or coffee or maybe some milk. Then walk away.

"I train at noon. And after training, I eat a light meal at two.

"If you're not going to fight too soon, run, but not too hard. Go to the gym regularly and train and keep in shape, but, again, not too hard. Always save some energy for the fight. And let me say this, being in shape is a reward in itself, not to mention the reward of being better able to win a fight. But being in shape is a reward in itself.

"There is no better feeling than being in top physical condition. It's euphoric. After just five or six weeks of jogging three or four miles and doing an hour or so of other exercises every day, you feel like a new person. Even after a good run, I feel revitalized. But after I really get in shape, my whole body glows in the dark. I don't catch colds. The food and water go down better. I sleep like a baby. My thinking is crystal clear, and I can remember and plan what I have to do faster and quicker. My sinuses are all clean and open. I don't get headaches. I'm relaxed. It's a feeling I want to always be able to enjoy."

chapter five

mastering the defense

Perhaps the easiest thing in boxing is to throw a punch. Anybody can do that. But what separates winners from losers is defense. The winners usually get hit the least and manage to stay out of trouble.

Jack Johnson, Jack Dempsey, Joe Louis, Sugar Ray Robinson, Archie Moore, Ernie Terrell, and Muhammad Ali all became winning boxers because they were superior defensive fighters. They hit their opponents either more or better than their opponents hit them. Ali, in fact, has been famous for pointing to his face and emphasizing how unmarked and "beautiful" it is. And after most of his fights, it was easy to tell who had lost: the guy with the puffy eye, bleeding nose, and deep cut over or under the eye.

If you want to become a winning boxer, place top training priority on defense. I always emphasize defense before offense because a good trainer is more concerned that his fighter not get hurt than that he hurt the other guy. Don't try to impress people with how well you can take a punch. There's no glory in taking a punch. The more punches you take, the greater your chances of losing, and the shorter your career will be.

CONDITIONING IS BEST DEFENSE

The best general defense against getting hit and beaten is to be in shape. When you are in top physical condition, you have optimum control of your body and your reflexes. You can act and react with maximum speed and quickness. You can out-think your opponent, be more perceptive about what he is doing or planning to do, and when you do get stung by a punch your recovery time is very quick.

Physical conditioning is so important to effective defense that I believe a fighter in top shape is almost impossible to knock out unless he doesn't see what hits him. If he can see a punch coming, in a decisive split second he can adjust and do whatever is necessary to get out of the way or minimize its impact.

Being in top condition means you'll be able to bob and weave at your best, move around the ring, avoid being cornered, and tire out your opponent. It means you'll enjoy a longer fighting career, too. Archie Moore is a textbook example here. He scored a record 141 knockouts in his career, was light heavyweight champion for roughly ten years, and was an active pro fighter for twenty-seven years because he combined excellent physical condition with strong defensive skills.

Moore was perfect at bobbing and weaving, and he also introduced the "armadillo" defense that still is the talk of boxing pundits. He'd go into this "armadillo" defense by crossing his arms, pressing them against his head with his elbows pointed out, his shoulders hunched against his jaw, and his chin tucked into his chest. This defense made Moore's head impregnable and tired out many fighters who tried to punch through it. Once they had tired, Moore would cut loose with some whopping punches of his own to score another KO.

STANCE AND MOVEMENT

The firm foundation of any boxing defense (or offense) is the boxer's stance—the way he positions his feet on the canvas. Proper stance results in sturdy balance, and balance enables a fighter to do almost anything he wants to do with his body.

There is no single stance that is best for every fighter. But the winning boxer at least knows and uses the classic straight-up stance: left foot out flat and slightly turned in, right foot at least twelve to eighteen inches back and resting on the ball of the foot, body weight concentrated on the left foot. As far as upper body form is concerned, one's arms and fists should be held up to throw punches. Elbows are kept in for defense. Chin is tucked into the hollow of the shoulders and head leans toward the left shoulder, which is slightly hunched against the chin.

In this stance, the fighter takes short sliding steps with his left foot while pushing off from the ball of his right foot. Avoid standing flat-footed, bringing your feet too close together, or crossing them. The proper foot placement and movement gives the fighter a necessary blend of balance and bounce.

With balance, you can avoid punches and also throw your own with maximum efficiency. The left foot planted flat bolsters balance. The right foot resting on the ball provides bounce or resilience so that when the fighter is hit, his body can give a little—the right foot serving as a sort of shock absorber to reduce the impact of the opponent's punch.

After mastering the basic straight-up stance, the fighter should try other techniques and settle on the one that is most comfortable and effective for his build, his size, and his physical capabilities.

If you're a short fighter in the mold of Floyd Patterson or Joe Frazier, you may reject the straight-up stance for a crouch, making yourself a smaller target. And you may bob and weave a lot to make yourself a more elusive one, too.

The classic straight-up stance is the foundation of a fighting defense and offense. For right-handers, the left foot is normally flat and forward, the right foot trailing roughly eighteen inches behind with the heel slightly raised. There is no perfect stance. Use the one that best balances you to hit and get out of trouble.

DEFENSE AGAINST PUNCHES

Sooner or later, you fighters will get hit. The later the better. But the sooner you learn how to defend yourself against punches, the quicker you will advance toward winning boxing.

Basic defensive moves against punches include: blocking, ducking or slipping, and clinching.

Blocking

Use your palms or the sides of your fists to brush jabs, straight hands, and crosses off to the side. This is also called parrying.

Picking off punches is one defensive tactic. The fighter uses his palm or the side of his fist to brush aside his opponent's punches.

Use your arms and elbows to block hooks and body shots. Try to use one arm so that your other can be free to counter. Blocking punches is the least desirable defense because being hit anywhere by a strong slugger can subject you to injury, and arms that absorb hooks can become too tired and sore to counterpunch. Fists and wrists also can be fractured when trying to stop head-on punches.

Ducking or Slipping

Crouch under, or step to the side of, advancing punches to evade them. This is also called bobbing and weaving. It is the most desirable defensive maneuver because it spares you contact with your opponent's punching power and leaves both your arms free to counterpunch. Avoiding punches altogether may also allow the opponent's momentum to throw him off balance and open him up for a good counterpunch. Remember, however, to move inside the opposing punch. Move to the right to slip a right punch, and to the left to slip a left punch. When this is done, even if there is some connection, your movement in the direction of—or rolling with—the punch diminishes its impact.

Clinching

Tying your opponent up, using your arms to hug his arms so that he can't hit you, is usually your best move when you're in trouble. It is limited, to be sure, because the referee will break it up, but it can give you a valuable few seconds to regain your balance and a clear mind if ever you are hurt by a punch. It can help you survive a round and hold onto a lead in points and victory. Clinching also can help you rest to keep from running out of gas.

All these methods, however, are useless if you do not possess sharp detection skills and a keen ability to anticipate. At all times Think! Think! Think! Be on the lookout for whatever your opponent is going to do. Also, keep your cool. Often you will find yourself fighting guys who use dirty tactics to try to

Clinching is another popular form of defense, especially for a fighter who is hurt. It can provide a precious few seconds to help the fighter clear his head. The referee will break a clinch because it is a form of holding, which is illegal.

anger you into forgetting your battle plan. But once you're angry, and fight like you're angry, you'll find yourself wild, erratic, and often exposed to being knocked out. Pay attention to your opponent. Don't ever let him out of your sight.

Former world heavyweight champion Patterson said he looked at his opponent's chest, other fighters may look at their opponent's eyes or stomach. All are reliable indicators of a fighter's real movement because they go where the fighter goes. If you try to concentrate on your opponent's moveable parts—his shoulders, head, arms, and legs—you set yourself up to be faked and possibly knocked out.

One good tip about the moveable body parts, however, is that they often telegraph your opponent's punches. A pulling back of the fist, a shrug of the shoulder, a moving forward of the chin—any movement that precedes the actual throwing of a punch is a telegram. Proper reading of such telegrams will help you anticipate the punch, prepare to slip it, and counter with a punch of your own.

TRAINER IS PART OF DEFENSE

Your trainer also is an invaluable part of your defense. His knowledge and skills can help keep you out of trouble, and can rescue you when you do get into trouble. Of course, the value of the trainer increases with his knowledge, skills, and experience. Having an inexperienced, ignorant trainer who is either too quiet or too loud is a tremendous liability, no matter how good a friend he may be. I've seen many fights, which should have been won, lost because the trainer didn't know what he was doing.

Bad trainers usually announce themselves by easily and quickly losing their tempers—arguing with or hollering at their fighters in an insulting way. This may be good for the trainer's ego—showing the people that he's the big, bad boss—but it certainly can demoralize a fighter. Moreover, the mistakes that the bad-tempered trainer is decrying so loudly are the same mistakes that he saw in the gym and failed to correct, due either to his laziness or his ignorance.

One favorite ego trip that bad trainers take is to ridicule, and seemingly disown, a fighter when he makes a mistake and gets hit hard. Some will holler something like, "See! I told you not to do that! That's what you get when you don't do what I tell you. Now don't do that anymore." Then when the fighter has his opponent in trouble, the trainer takes credit for it by screaming, "That's right! Now you're doing what I told you! That's it!"

But when good trainers see things from ringside during a fight—certain weakness in you or in your opponent—they will call your attention to them in a way that does not degrade you or exalt them. A good trainer can diagnose style and strategy and warn you when your opponent is setting traps.

A good trainer can usually tell when you're behind on points and will help you adopt the right strategy to get those points back. A good trainer serving in your corner will also be a very good cut man: if you're cut, and it's not serious enough to stop the fight, he will be able to stop the bleeding in as little as ten seconds and make the necessary temporary repair to enable you to go back out and fight.

51

A good trainer takes excellent care of his fighter between rounds. He rests him, treats his wounds, and, during those crucial sixty seconds, gives him the knowledge and inspiration to win.

I always developed a lot of special code words with my fighters so that I could give them instructions during a fight without letting the opponent's corner know what we were talking about. For example, former world junior welterweight champion Eddie Perkins and I would call a straight jab "cobra" and a counterpunch against a jab "mongoose." When I'd see that the time was ripe for jabbing, I'd holler "cobra!" When I'd see certain punches telegraphed by an opponent, I'd holler "mongoose!" to tell him to anticipate the punch and get set to counterpunch. Sometimes we'd switch the meaning of the terms just to keep people from learning them.

The minute between rounds is crucial. A good trainer will budget that minute to maximize rest for his fighter and at the same time to do and say whatever is necessary to help the fighter win. A good trainer is calm, always concerned, but positive. He radiates confidence and uses psychology to get the most out of his fighter.

OFFENSE IS BEST DEFENSE?

Defense is not all defense; it is partly offense.

Having a strong offense, especially as a counterpuncher, makes your opponent think twice about throwing punches. He realizes that when he misses, he may pay a high price if you connect with your counterpunch. Fighters who are not respected as sluggers certainly cannot stir fear and respect in their opponents, who will feel freer to gamble by throwing haymakers at random.

I would not go so far as to say one's offense is his best defense. That is absurd in boxing. One certainly has to depend upon more than his offense to protect him. For example, Sonny Liston scored a quick knockout over Floyd Patterson, who was a smaller fighter, simply by overpowering him. George Foreman did the same to Joe Frazier.

Liston and Foreman commanded tremendous advantage in physical size and strength and went all out early to overwhelm Patterson and Frazier. In truth, though, Liston and Foreman were weak defensive fighters in situations in which they fought people their own size. It took Muhammad Ali to prove this. They were stronger than he, but not much bigger. And Ali was a defensive genius who was agile and quick enough to evade their powerful punches. He'd feint and sucker them into wasting their offensive strengths in the early stages. Then he'd prove their lack of defense by scoring stunning knockouts.

Don't ever consider your offense to be your best defense. Your best defense is your best defense. But your total defense certainly includes your offense. Be able both to counterpunch and to be the aggressor. Let your opponent know that you can do more than just duck and clinch.

53

chapter six

mastering the offense

In boxing, as in competitive team sports, offense is the most glamorous part of a match.

Basketball fans like to see their favorite team score 100 points, complete with slam dunks and sky hooks. Hockey fans love to see the slap shot zipping through the enemy goalie's legs. Football fans go wild when their team connects on a "bomb." And baseball fans become hysterical after a grand-slam home run.

In boxing, jackhammer jabs snapping back your opponent's head will bring a few cheers. Connecting on a right cross to stagger your opponent will trigger even more cheers. Then when you floor him with a mighty left hook, the crowd jumps to its feet and explodes with cheers.

54

The glamour of the knockout will inspire many of you to place most if not all of your emphasis on scoring knockouts. But hunting knockouts is not the best offensive formula for winning boxing. The more you gamble for the knockout, the more you gamble on suffering the same.

Your best approach to a winning offense is to comprehensively master the total offense. Learn the basic punches. Use them. If a chance for a knockout comes, take it. But don't make the knockout your principal objective.

The basic punches are the jabs, the hooks, and the crosses—all from the left or the right.

THE JAB

The basic building block of a winning offense is the jab, which also answers to the name of "stick." "Stick" is indeed a graphic description of the jab. One jabs by simply sticking his fist into his opponent's face. Consequently, the jab serves as a defensive stick keeping your opponent at bay, and as an offensive stick poking or needling your foe toward defeat. When the trainer hollers "Stick 'im! Stick and move! Stick 'im!" he means for his fighter to jab. In itself, the jab is not famed as a knockout punch. It is a setup punch for the heavier artillery—the crosses and the hooks. But if executed successfully and consistently, it can win a fight on points or by inflicting a cut that can lead to a TKO (technical knockout) decision.

The jab flows naturally from the classic straight-up stance. The left arm is slightly extended and cocked for release. The fighter has only to shoot his arm and fist straight out while propelling the punch with the weight of his body. The fist only needs to move eight to twelve inches to land an effective jab.

The jab is not just a function of arm, wrist, and fist. The bulk of the body comes into play as you put your weight behind it. Putting your weight behind your jab or any other punch will seem very awkward at first. It requires a sense of balance and coordination that you acquire by working out again and again against sparring partners and on the heavy bag.

55

Ernie Terrell, a former WBA heavyweight champion, fires his jab from the basic straight-up stance. He sticks out his left, thrusting his weight behind the punch. Immediately, he recoils into the basic stance to defend against counterpunches.

However, one way to get the feel of putting your weight behind your punches is to shoot out your hand toward a wall as if you are falling. Hit the wall as if it stopped you from falling, blocking or catching the forward flow of your body weight. Remember, you still would not fall if the wall were suddenly removed as you leaned forward because your left foot would still be planted on the canvas to support your body weight.

Also remember that the first part of your forward movement is your fist, not your foot. Any part of the body that moves before the actual punch is a telegram. The left foot moving first indicates that a jab is set to follow. One way to move your left foot before the jab without telegraphing the punch is to dance. For example, Ali prancing and shuffling and dangling his hands low makes it a little difficult for opponents to know just when his jab will follow a certain foot movement.

THE HOOK

While the jab contributes to most of the TKOs because of its ability to cut a fighter's face, especially around the eyes, the hook is the devastating punch that stretches out the opponent for the count and then some.

Like the jab, it can be thrown without a whole lot of room. The picture of a fighter drawing his fist back as far as he can and then cutting loose with a punch is not the classic hook. If anything, it's a telegram asking for a knockout. The classic hook can knock a guy out after traveling a mere twelve inches if a fighter's weight is properly placed behind it.

With the hook, the entire weight of the body is brought into play. A hook does not involve a forward lunge the way a jab thrown on the move does. As you throw a hook, you simply turn and lift your weight into it. This kind of propulsion has the effect of prying your opponent loose from the floor. Thus, the knockout hook often is accurately described as having knocked an opponent "clear off his feet."

Since it is usually thrown in close, the hook can easily be thrown with either hand. Right-handers are naturally partial to

57

The left hook, a powerful close and intermediate range punch, starts with the left fist pulled slightly in. Then it is flung across the front. The body twists as its weight shifts from left foot to right foot, powering the follow-through. The right hook is done the same way, but the direction of movement is reversed.

the left hook and throw it with more power because the bulk of the right-hander's body weight is already on his left foot, allowing him to push off and shift to the right as his body turns from left to right in the direction of the punch. The right hook is administered by shifting the body weight from right foot to left as body turns likewise.

THE UPPERCUT

It's practically impossible to throw an effective uppercut without being in close. It must come up through the center of the body because its main target is the opponent's chin, one of his more sensitive areas. As with the hook, the body is shifting and pushing up, propelling the uppercut.

The right uppercut is a very effective infighting weapon. It often starts from a crouch position, then comes up through the middle of the opponent, aimed for either his body or his chin.

Because it is a punch that comes up from your center of gravity and does not impart momentum to the side, and because it is thrown during infighting and is likely to connect with some part of the opponent's body, the uppercut causes less imbalance in the follow-through than any other punch.

When the uppercut is whipped or slung into the body or into the head of a crouching opponent, it is then described as a bolo punch—one that Kid Gavilan and Beau Jack made famous. Many right-handers will find the right bolo punch effective

against southpaws. Right bolos against southpaws can serve the same purpose as jabs in that they can open things up for other punches like right hooks, or even left hooks when a southpaw starts favoring your right bolos.

THE COMBINATION

A combination is two or more punches thrown in succession. It is usually triggered by a jab. One popular combination is a left

A combination is two or more punches thrown in succession. Speed is the key to successful combination punching.

jab immediately followed by a right cross. Another is a left hook followed by a right hook followed by a left hook. Still another is two or more hooks thrown by the same hand.

Quickness obviously is the key to the effectiveness and versatility of the combination. The quicker the puncher, the greater number of punches, of various kinds, he can throw in succession. The combination is highly valuable to the winning boxer since few boxers get the opportunity to knock out their opponent with one punch. Most fighters have the ability to do this, but seldom get the opportunity.

Combinations are safer to use than single punches when trying for a knockout. A fighter is seldom more vulnerable to being knocked out than when he misses a punch. Throwing and missing haymakers forces you too much off balance and leaves you wide open for a knockout counterpunch. Missed haymakers can also result in strained muscles or even shoulder separations.

INFIGHTING

When you sting your opponent with a punch or when he starts getting tired, he will either clinch or cover himself up on the ropes and bob and weave. When this happens you must have the ability to finish your opponent off at close range before his head clears. Combinations of hooks and uppercuts to the head and body are the main weapons in this kind of situation. The key is to keep your opponent from tying up both your arms and leaning on you so that you cannot punch. He will try to grab a few precious seconds of rest and at the same time tire you as you support his weight.

Many opponents who see that they are heavier and stronger than you, but not as quick, will use clinching and leaning tactics to tire you out and slow you down until they can catch you and overpower you. Some referees will allow you to push your man off when he tries to clinch too much. If so, do this and throw your shots. Also, when your opponent tries to put his weight on you, let your body give. Don't push against him or try to hold him up. Move back, make him walk into you, and use your power to punch. Trying to push against a leaning and clinching opponent decreases the body weight you have to put behind your punches.

The heavy bag is the main training tool used to develop infighting techniques. Practice swinging it and punching it, pushing it away and punching it as it comes in.

Watch out for butts when infighting. Keep your head up. Opponents who crouch under you, rolling their heads, are coiled for a quick butt that can open fight-stopping cuts anywhere on your face—especially on your eyes. Don't infight with your face down. Of course, it is illegal to bring one's head or shoulder up under the chin of one's opponent, but a fighter can do this before a referee sees it and may get away with a decisive butt or two. Also, beware when breaking a clinch. Some fighters will take advantage of the split second following a break to hit you with a quick punch. It is usually best, then, to let the referee come between you and separate you.

FEINTING

Feinting is using any kind of body movement to deceive your opponent and coax him into providing an opening for you to score. It is making your opponent think you are going to throw a right when you are going to throw a left. It is making your opponent think you're hurt when you just want him to come within range of your left hook.

Used properly, feints can provide the same advantage that jabs do—making the opponent swing, and miss, leaving himself open for a solid punch or combination. However, don't be too quick to anticipate that an opponent will go for your fake. Sometimes he won't, and you may fake yourself and possibly suffer the same damage you were intending to inflict.

Feinting is an excellent psychological weapon, too. It can confuse your opponent so that he never knows when you are going to do what. The left jab is the chief tool for setting up an opponent for a strong right hand. If the jab lands consistently and effectively, it may coax an opponent into concentrating too much of his defense against the jab, thus opening himself for a fake of a left jab followed by a quick right hook.

The first round or two is usually the best time to test market your fakes if you are going to test market them. See what your man will go for before you commit yourself to punching off fakes.

ALL AREAS SENSITIVE

Some boxing theorists put a lot of stock in so-called "sensitive areas" and physical targets most vulnerable to attack. These include the frontal rim of the chin, the nerve center at the base of the nose, the solar plexis (where the front ribs meet), the temples, the eyes (especially when cut), the area over and under the heart, the bottom rim of the ribs, the side edges of the jawbone, and the so-called funny bone (just above the elbow). I agree that these areas are sensitive. But I also agree with former WBA heavyweight champion Ernie Terrell's analysis. I offer it to you as food for thought.

"Any area becomes a sensitive area when you hit it hard and long enough. A guy who is a hard hitter can hit you in the arm a couple of times and deaden it. He can hit you a certain way on your wrist and sprain or break it. If there is a so-called sensitive target, it is any area above the belt that's open for you to hit. It is true that Ali has inspired a big generation of head-hunters—fighters whose main target is the opponent's head. And almost all knockouts result from blows to the head that either knock the fighter unconscious or injure him so badly, the doctor rules him too physically endangered to continue. But if the head isn't open, then hit the stomach, hit the chest; hit whatever part you can. Be aggressive and score as many points as you can."

chapter seven

scoring with the system

The aspiring winning boxer must understand that boxing reflects the human society of which he is an integral part. The sport is a structure with its own culture, history, and administration. It has its own laws, but it must also adhere to and abide by the various legal, moral, and social laws of America and the world.

As soon as one commits himself to becoming a winning fighter, he is informed of various laws by the athletic commission which licenses him, the trainer who trains him, the manager who guides his professional career, and the promoter who provides the market for his entertaining skills.

In boxing, there is no central governing agency. There is much division and confusion; so much that in many cases there is more than one world champion in a single weight division. It has been this way for years. Thus, a fighter must learn to cope with division, confusion, and near anarchy as he struggles to climb to the top. Look at winning boxing as a game, one which you win by scoring points in all facets of the sport.

TRAINER, MANAGER, PROMOTER

The trainer, manager, and promoter play vital roles in the guidance of your career. You score points by getting along with them.

The trainer is usually closest to the boxer because he spends most time working personally with him. He is paid either by the manager, who usually pays your training expenses and gets a percentage of your purses, or directly by you. Sometimes you may argue with your trainer over strategy. But always listen to your trainer, respect him for his wisdom, and try to stay in harmony with him.

Second closest to you is your manager. Fighters usually have conflicts with managers before trainers because managers exer-

cise control over money. They have the power to sign for the fighter, agree to his fights and his purses. With such rights spelled out in a contract, he can hold up your purse until he gets his cut, which can vary from nothing to everything, depending upon how much money he claims you owe him. When a fighter ends up penniless and with a bad record, the manager is usually to blame. In many cases, the blame is deserved.

The promoter usually works with your manager. They agree on your opponent, your purse, and the date and place you will fight. But you have an obligation to the promoter to fulfill your contract by fighting. Not showing up for a fight gives you a bad name, brands you as unreliable, and eventually discourages promoters from signing you for a fight.

Trying to break a valid contract with your manager or with a promoter is also discouraged. As in other sports, athletes often consider contracts pieces of paper that they sign simply for convenience, and they try to break them whenever they feel like it. Often, a fighter will sign a contract with such-and-such a manager, let the manager support him, move him up to get a shot at the title and the big money, then want to cut the manager out of the contract and keep all the money for himself.

Put up a good fight. You owe it to the promoter who put you on the card and to the commission that has graded your past performances. Lying on the ropes, covering up and refusing to fight, can not only end in defeat but also in suspension and a move by the commission to hold up your purse.

JUDGES

The judges often seem to be spectators who are underrated by fighters. I'm talking about fighters who play to the crowd. They come to showboat and thrill the crowd, not as much with actual fighting as with flashy dress, gimmick punching, and gimmick footwork.

You must be aware that the judges do not award points for your colorful trunks, robe, or shoes. They do not award points for fantastic footwork, such as your ability to duplicate the Ali shuffle. They are not impressed with your ability to take a punch, or out-talk your opponent, or throw more punches than he does.

Judges award points for the following: effective clean punches to the front and sides of the head and body; avoidance of or defense against punches; initiative; and good sportsmanship. Fighters are docked points for fouls.

Boxing fouls include the following: kicking with the knee; hitting an opponent when he's down; butting with head, elbows, or forearms; hitting an opponent below the belt; holding an opponent's arm; rabbit-punching (hitting an opponent behind the head); stepping on an opponent's foot and hitting him; hanging onto an opponent. If a foul is ruled serious and blatantly intentional, the referee can disqualify you, stop the

In your efforts to impress the people who come to see you fight, don't forget the judge. He is the main person the winning boxer strives to impress.

fight, and hand your opponent the victory no matter who was leading in points.

The most popular scoring formulas are the ten-point must and the five-point must. The winner gets the maximum ten or five, while the loser gets whatever less than the maximum the judges thinks he deserves. The fighter who totals the most points after the fight wins.

Another scoring method is by rounds—the fighter who wins the most number of rounds wins the fight. Still another method is the Soctron system—each judge has a computer he uses to award points each time a fighter lands an effective punch. The fighter with the most points wins the match.

Bear in mind, however, that not all judges are honest. You owe it to yourself to try to score as many points as you can, avoiding close fights as best you can, especially on the road. There *are* hometown decisions. And often, if you are not an overwhelming winner, you will get robbed.

Butting with head.

69

Elbowing.

Rabbit punching.

the system

Kneeing.

Sticking thumb in
opponent's eye.

71

Hitting opponent
below the belt.

Stepping on
opponent's feet
and hitting him.

72

the system

Rubbing glove laces in opponent's face.

Kidney punching.

Holding onto your
opponent.

BOXING COMMISSION

Your local boxing commission is your friend—at least it should
be. Abide by its laws. Report to the weigh-in at the weight you
were contracted to fight at. Report early to the site where you
are to fight so that you can get dressed, get your hands taped,
and get approved for the bout.

Taping or bandaging rules differ. But a standard limit on
taping is not more than twelve feet of two-inch, soft bandage for

all weights. Some commissions will permit nine feet of one-inch, zinc oxide, plaster tape for weights through middleweight and eleven feet of similar tape for light-heavyweights and heavy-weights.

The handwrap is predominately gauze with shreds of tape, one-eighth-inch wide, between the fingers to hold the gauze. Usually no tape is permitted on the knuckles because taped

Before each bout, your hands must be properly bandaged. Get a veteran to do it if you can. The boxing commission approves bandaged hands to be sure that excess tape is not used. Excess tape, especially when wet, hardens the fists and causes injury.

knuckles get wet, become hard, and can feel almost like brass knuckles when one is hit with them. The commission approves each fighter's bandaged hands before he takes the ring.

Remember that your chief second is allowed to take the following into your corner: sterile cotton, white petroleum jelly (for lubricating skin to minimize and treat cuts), sterile gauze in sealed packets, surgical spirits (not mentholated), blunt-edged surgical scissors, swab sticks, solution of adrenalin, water in taped bottle, spit bucket, towel, and ice. Smelling salts, alcohol, or any controlled drugs are absolutely forbidden in a fighter's corner.

Boxing commissions expect a good performance from you each time you fight. They grade you and if you put forward a very poor performance or break a fight contract for no justifiable reason, they can suspend you. These are some of the things they do to prevent fighters from throwing fights. The commission thus looks unkindly on the following sorts of things: a fighter clinching too much and showing that he obviously is out of shape; a fighter committing blatant fouls; a fighter not attacking his opponent; a fighter taking a full ten-count on his knees, or jumping off the canvas obviously unhurt after being counted out; a fighter acting highly unusual, as if under the influence of a foreign substance.

Help the commission to keep boxing clean. If you are ever approached and offered money to throw a fight, report it to the boxing commission. If you know that someone else has thrown a fight, report this to the commission. Fixing fights destroys boxing.

THE PRESS

Good publicity will come to you when you consistently do well. Many fighters feel they deserve front-page coverage after one or two impressive wins. Some even try to intimidate the media into writing only good things about them. The press represents the eyes and ears of the public. Score points with the press by being polite and honest. Since boxing is an individual sport, many fighters are prone to lie to newsmen about their age and records to boost their egos and make people think that they are better than they really are. Some fighters even lie about past opponents, claiming they have beaten certain ranked fighters. Once you are caught in a lie, newsmen will avoid you or minimize their involvement with you.

If you are asked a question for publication, always try to be as truthful as you can in your answers. If you don't know the answer, say so. On the other hand, don't let newsmen put words

Always try to accommodate the press. It is your pipeline to the people, and you need the people. They are your market. Be courteous and, especially, be honest about yourself and about others. Lying to make yourself look good makes you look bad when the truth is learned. If you don't know the answer to certain questions, be honest.

in your mouth. Some newsmen will come into your locker after or before a fight with their stories already written and quotes already attributed to you. Then they ask you questions in such a way that you confirm their prewritten quotes.

When you are easy to talk to and truthful in what you say, and if you have talent, you will get publicity. And the more

77

publicity you get, the more the public will get behind you and help assure you of title shots when you deserve them.

It helps to keep account of your records. Know your basic background. It would even help your progress as a winning boxer to keep pictures and a brief biography of yourself for promoters and newsmen to use when they want to push you. Few things frustrate a newsman more than talking to a fighter who doesn't know how long he's been fighting, what his amateur record was, when he turned pro, what his pro record is, or whom, when, and where he last fought.

Remember, when you score points with the press and get good publicity, you likewise get points with the public and build a following. And that's who really pays you, your fans. The more people you bring into the arena, the more money the promoter is obliged to pay you.

It is important, then, that you maintain a positive, wholesome, public image—one that people would like their children to emulate. Stay away from cigarettes and don't drink anything other than an occasional beer, and do that in private. Don't ever involve yourself with any kind of drug to help you fight. When you have to have drugs to fight, you are a loser. Hang it up! Be involved in the community in some helpful way. Working with youngsters is a natural since the winning boxer is looked upon as a model human being who maintains high physical and moral standards.

BACKERS

Winning boxers inspire investors. Muhammad Ali and Joe Frazier are excellent examples of fighters who got investors behind them—investors who paid their salaries thus enabling them to train full-time.

This is the ideal way to pursue winning boxing: training full-time. Working a regular job and then coming to the gym already tired burns a fighter out quickly, both mentally and physically. Your reflexes are slow in a sparring session, your timing is off, and you subject yourself to more punishment than you normally would.

But once you get the backing, be careful about what kind of contract you sign. Have your own lawyer and your trainer and some relative help spell out the specifics of such a contract. You don't want to sign yourself away for life, giving investors total control over your career and your money.

And once you sign a contract, be true to it. You owe it to your trainers to train and stay in shape. This way you're better able to give them a return on their investment. After you fight, you may take off a couple of days. I'm not saying that you should always stay in tip-top fighting shape. But it's in your best interest to maintain the best shape you can. You ought to maintain at least eighty percent of your peak condition so that you can fight efficiently with just a few days' notice.

With a boxer, there really is no such thing as an "off season." Boxing is a year-round sport. So you must stay in shape year-round. If you live in an area where the winters are pretty fierce, just increase your workouts in the gym. Greater emphasis on physical fitness has resulted in the construction of many well-equipped gyms with indoor running tracks, etc. Weather can never be an excuse for a so-called fighter to be out of shape. Always want to fight and be able to fight.

You'll find that many times a scheduled fighter will pull out of a match for some reason or another and the promoter will need a replacement. Many fighters have gotten their biggest breaks this way, fighting a name fighter as a replacement and knocking him out. By the same token, many fighters have missed these opportunities or failed to take good advantage of them because they were out of shape.

You should never stray more than five or six pounds away from your fighting weight as long as you are active. It's easy to gain weight, but very hard to lose it.

chapter eight

creative strategy

In war, nothing is more dreaded and destructive than the "surprise attack." The same applies in boxing. The element of surprise—whether a new punch, a new defense, a new move or rhythm—can confuse an opponent, throw him off guard, and set him up for a knockout.

On the other hand, the fighter who, let's say, always leads with his left and follows with his right makes it easier for an opponent to beat him. The key word here is "always." If a fighter "always" does anything in the ring the same way, his style becomes predictable and he becomes prey for a decisive counterpunch. That's why you'll so often hear me hollering to my fighters, "Mix it up! Mix up your punches!" I've seen from

Ali practices his rope-a-dope tactic during a sparring session. He surprised George Foreman with it in Zaire, Africa, suckering Foreman into punching himself tired. Ali them proceeded to knock out the weary Foreman, winning the title for the third time. Rope-a-doping, however, is not for everybody—especially not for beginners.

experience that too much of anything, no matter how good it is, eventually becomes too bad for the fighter.

If three-time, world heavyweight boxing champion Muhammad Ali has taught us anything, he has taught us that success in boxing depends on creative strategy—the ability to come up with a new technique that your opponent doesn't expect and to devise fresh strategy each fight to exploit your opponent's weaknesses.

Ali surprised Sonny Liston twice, once to win and once to successfully defend the world crown. He blew Liston's mind with dance and lightning body moves in the first fight, frustrating Liston into a shoulder separation. In the second fight, Ali unleashed a "secret anchor punch" that knocked Liston out. Ali said he created this punch with help from comedian Stepin Fetchit. "It's a chop, so fast you can't see it," Ali described it. "It's got a twist to it."

Zora Foley, whom many called a boxing scientist, studied Ali fight films again and again and thought he knew all there was to know about Ali. But in their 1967 bout, Ali kept Foley off balance with an unusual blend of horseplay (standing still, lowering his fists, and daring Foley to hit him), jackhammer jabs, and "phantom" punches before knocking him out in the seventh round with a right cross.

Finally, in the 1975 jungle rumble in Zaire, Africa, George Foreman was just plain unprepared to deal with Ali's deceptive "rope-a-dope" tactic. Ali shielded his head with his fists and let Foreman tire himself out flailing body shots.

NEW TACTICS TAKE TIME

The same tactics won't work the same magic against every opponent. You beginning and intermediate fighters—don't try any "rope-a-doping" or dancing with your fists low. It could be suicide for you. Don't try these tactics in a fight just because you saw Ali use them on television. Ali didn't perfect these tactics and skills overnight. He was years into his pro career before he dared to use them, and he didn't use them until he had

The Ali shuffle was a dash of fast footwork that momentarily surprised foes, threw them off balance, and, at the same time, thrilled the crowd. It was a result of Ali's creative strategy.

experimented with them against foes less awesome than the likes of Liston, Foley, and Foreman.

You don't have to be a copycat to be successful. Be creative. Each fighter is a research and development scientist, and the ring is his laboratory. You have the intelligence, individuality, and the physical skills and dimensions to pioneer new tactics that will make you a winner and enrich the fistic craft.

By all means, learn the traditional basics covered in earlier chapters. You may even learn a little Ali, a little Sugar Ray Robinson, or a little Joe Frazier if you have the body for their styles. But don't try to pattern yourself totally after anybody else. Be creative!

How do you be creative? Simply by applying yourself in the gym, especially against your sparring partners. Find out what you can do with your body that others can't do with theirs. You may be taking for granted some skills of your own that would make Ali, Larry Holmes, and all previous champions look like babies in comparison.

Is your footwork unusually good, and does it consistently throw your opponents off balance? Is your upper body movement exceptionally quick so that foes can't hit you if you don't want them to? Do you have uncommon power in your punches, or do you find it easy to hit your opponents? If so, work on these talents, perfect them and try something new with them.

EVERY FIGHTER IS UNIQUE

If there seems to be nothing at all unusual about your size, strength, or other capabilities, do the best you can with what you have; you'll discover your individuality that way. It is not necessary that you *try* to be different. You are already unique. No two fighters are exactly the same. Every boxer has something different about him. There are things he can do better than other boxers. A good trainer looks out for these things; he helps a fighter find them after long, hard hours in the gym.

Bear in mind that unusual punches and moves are not always good. Some are bad for a fighter and should be corrected. That's where a good trainer comes in. You want your fighter to be creative and to find out what he can do best. But the trainer's job is to look at his fighter's style objectively and make him change if it isn't making him a winner. A fighter by himself may not be objective. He'll keep bad habits for selfish reasons, until they get him beaten. And even then, he'll sometimes make excuses to justify his mistakes.

Once you creatively come up with a technique that you feel comfortable with and which is effective in winning fights, be confident and use it with authority. But don't be too anxious to use it. Don't be so confident that you become cocky and think nobody can beat you. Take your time and be precise, especially if your "secret weapon" is a "new" punch. Practice so that you execute your punch perfectly.

DANGEROUS TO MISS

One of the most dangerous things you can do in a fight is take a big swing and miss. True, fighters often get away with missing haymakers. But missing a big punch is dangerous because you (1) expose your skills and (2) sacrifice much of your defense.

One of the keys that unlocks the door to a boxing victory is knowledge of an opponent's strengths and weaknesses. What kind of stuff does this guy have? What do I have to watch out for most? Is he in shape? How much punishment can he take? Can I risk taking a punch from him? Is this guy trying for a quick knockout? These are typical questions fighters ask themselves about each other at the start of a bout. And the fighter that throws the first punch gives the other fighter a headstart in getting such information.

This is not meant to discourage you from throwing the first punch. If the first punch is successful enough, it could be the only punch of the fight. Indeed, that's the way it was for Luke Capuano, promising young Chicago heavyweight, when he fought Cincinnati's Lemuel Moore in Chicago, October 25, 1978: "As soon as the opening bell sounded, this guy comes at me leading with his chin," said Capuano, who saluted that chin with a right cross to score a twelve-second knockout before a shocked Aragon Ballroom crowd. "That probably won't happen again in a thousand years."

If the punch is available, take it! Otherwise, realize that it isn't any automatic honor or prestige for a fighter to throw the first punch. A mark of inexperience is a fighter throwing—and missing—punches just to impress the press, thrill the crowd, or scare his opponent. Throwing punches that don't land is a waste of energy. It also invites such injuries as pulled muscles and shoulder separations. Save that energy! Don't throw a punch unless you intend to score with it. And don't show your opponent any more of your ability than you have to. Remember, you're not fighting to impress or to scare your opponent. You're fighting to beat him. You're fighting to win.

BEWARE OF COUNTERPUNCHES

Another key to a boxing victory is catching your opponent off balance. When a fighter misses a punch, he himself can become vulnerable, during his follow-through, to a solid counterpunch.

Some fighters score most of their points and win most of their fights on counterpunches. Ali, Jerry Quarry, Sugar Ray Robinson, Sugar Ray Leonard, Larry Holmes, and Ken Norton—all have distinguished themselves as top-of-the-line counterpunchers. All quick afist, they've answered many a missed punch with a knockout punch.

Imagine, for a moment, a slow-motion, instant replay of a missed—let's say—right hook. See how the swing pulls the fighter off balance. Notice how the fighter's arm is flung across his body leaving much of the right side of his head and body wide open.

True, a fighter can throw a punch, miss, and regain his balance and defensive stance in about a second. But in boxing, where quickness generally is more valuable than either power or speed, a knockout punch can be thrown in a split second.

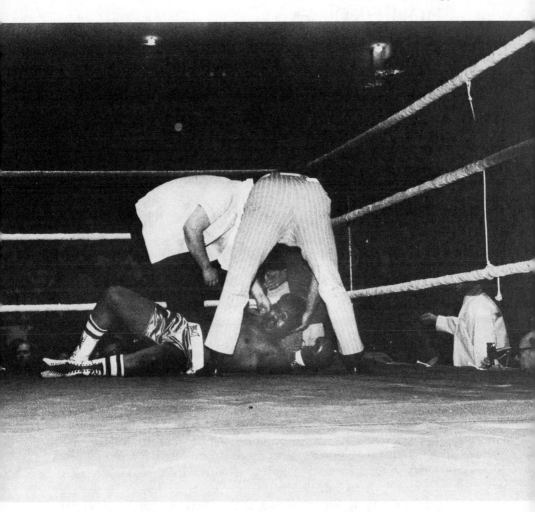

The fighter on the canvas made one mistake too many and got knocked out. Carson urges his fighters to "Think!" and make every move count toward victory. A lack of concentration in the ring, even for a split second, can make a loser out of you.

chapter nine

from rags to riches to rags

The majority of boxers have come from relatively poor back-grounds with dreams of winning a world title, striking it rich, and retiring in comfort for the rest of their lives. They have come into boxing literally hungry, and that hunger has brought out the best in them. This hunger—this matter-of-life-and-death kind of urgency—eventually matures into love: love of the ring, love of physical combat, love of being in excellent physical condition, love of having a real shot at becoming champion. Such love makes men dedicate themselves to training and becoming winners.

Any young man who dedicates himself to winning boxing, and does win, will eventually become rich. The radio, television, and movie industries have made it possible for boxers, even non-champions, to become multimillionaires with just one fight. The glamour of Muhammad Ali as the people's champion made million-dollar paydays for world heavyweight championship bouts a regular thing. In his career, Ali himself has grossed some $60 million in fight purses alone, not to mention the million or so dollars his popularity as champion has earned him in speaking engagements, public appearances, commercial endorsements, and movies.

WASTE LEADS TO POVERTY

Too many winning boxers have see-sawed from rags to riches, back to rags. Several of them rose from obscure poverty, became world champions and made a lot of money, only to tumble down and become forgotten has-beens struggling to pay the rent or drinking and panhandling on skid row.

There are reasons for this. Many of the fighters were poorly educated and entrusted their talent and money to fast-talking managers, promoters, or lawyers who exploited and mismanaged them. On the other hand, many fighters fearful of being cheated refused to listen to or trust anybody and ended up cheating themselves with unwise investments. They wasted their money on luxury cars, clothes, jewelry, hangers-on, wine, and women. Unfortunately, this has resulted in a stigma: champions are expected to drive big cars and throw money around until they become poor. I've even seen some fighters—some nonchampions—waste money like this after they've won a few fights. They want people to call them a big shot, so they flash money and waste it.

This book is aimed at helping you to become and remain a winning boxer. But the real goal of winning boxing is not confined to the ring; it includes the kind of life it produces for you and the kind of person it makes out of you. You should continue to be the kind of man that boxing makes you even after you leave the ring. In other words, "winning boxing" is not "winning boxing" if, in the end, it makes a loser out of you as a man. And any man who gets to the point where he can't stand on his own feet and has to beg money to survive—he is a loser as a man.

EDUCATION INVALUABLE

As a winning fighter you get a lot of help wasting money when you have some. A lot of people come up smiling, praising you and swearing they're your friends. Some tell you they know a can't-miss deal that will double your money. Some latch onto you for little odd jobs that don't need doing or that you could easily do for yourself. People who approach you this way are called hangers-on because they literally try to hang on and around you, hoping you'll throw some money their way.

Education will help you to withstand this kind of hypocrisy. It will help you to see through a lot of shady propositions. It will help you to budget and wisely invest your money. Education will help you realize that you don't have to wear diamond rings and spend money impressing people to be a champion. Education will help you realize that the little money you have won't last forever. It will help you not only to think for today, but also to prepare for tomorrow.

Get as much education as you can so that your life won't be totally dependent upon someone else's intelligence or lack of it. You can never have too much education as a boxer, but you can surely have too little of it. Lack of education has cost many fighters many dollars. Lack of education has cost many fighters their lives because they didn't know how to take care of themselves, how to think for themselves, or how to keep other people from influencing them to get mixed up with drugs, gambling, the bottle and what not.

Education also enables you to learn other skills, some of them more profitable and less dangerous than boxing. Few of you will get backers to finance your training and pay your living expenses so that you can train full-time. You will have to have another job to support you. The more education you have, the better the job you can qualify for, and the less desperate you'll be as a boxer. Desperate fighters will fight when they're out of shape, and will fight opponents they know they can't beat because they need the money and have no quicker way of getting it lawfully.

Desperate fighters also are often forced to fight when they are too old and their skills have left them. Some become professional punching bags and subject themselves to irreparable injuries because, as they say, they don't know anything else to do. Get an education so that you will never have to say such a thing.

LEARN TO SAVE AND INVEST

Most of you will not be fortunate enough to become a world champion and make a million dollars. When you start out fighting your four-rounders, you won't get more than $100 or $200 for each of your fights. But as soon as possible, try to save as much as you can. Get a routine together and put a certain amount in a savings account every so often. The more money you earn, the more base support you get from your manager or from private backers, the easier this will be.

Be careful about so-called big investments. Beware of strangers who come to you as soon as you get a little money and try to talk you into some get-rich-quick scheme. Study investments, have some knowledgeable relative or, if you can afford one, a lawyer help you.

One of the safest investments going these days is land. Buying a house or just a piece of land can profit you a lot because real estate prices are going up fast. Another thing about land is that it's hard to steal. Diamond rings, watches, big cars, fancy clothes—they can all be stolen easily. Some of these luxury items also can be destroyed by fire. But the value of land can endure fire better than that of any other property.

index